Celebrate Jesus
Activity Book

CONTENTS

NOTE TO PARENTS

The *Celebrate Jesus Activity Book*, is geared towards young children and can be used by individuals or groups of children in schools or clubs. It is ideal for Christmas, Easter or any season.

The stories remind children of Jesus' birth, amazing miracles, crucifixion, ascension and close return.

Activities are designed to encourage creativity and participation on the part of the child. The materials for each activity consist of inexpensive items, and odds and ends found in the home.

Instructions and diagrams are easy to follow, however parental assistance may be required. Children will enjoy hours of fun making gifts for friends and family.

So . . . let the fun begin.

This sign indicates that parental help is need for this part of the activity

For David Sr., Melissa and David Jr.

LEARN ABOUT... JESUS, SON OF GOD

This story can be found in the Bible in Luke 1: 26 - 38 and Luke 2: 1 - 7

Mary was getting married to Joseph, the local carpenter. One day, something strange happened in Mary's house. An angel called Gabriel appeared to her.

'You have been chosen to have God's Son, Jesus who will reign forever,' said the angel.

'How will this happen? I am not married yet,' Mary asked the angel.

'By God's amazing power.'

Mary was happy. But what would Joseph say? Mary told Joseph everything. Joseph was worried because the neighbours would think he was the father.

An angel appeared to Joseph in a dream.

'Don't be afraid, Joseph. Mary is pregnant with God' s Son. He will save many from their sins.'

Caesar Augustus, the Roman ruler wanted every person to go to their own town to be registered. He wanted to know who lived in his land. Mary and Joseph lived in Nazareth. They had to go to Bethlehem to register. Mary rode on a donkey. It was almost time for Jesus to be born.

Joseph knocked on a door.

'Sorry. We're full,' the innkeeper said.

'My wife is about to have a baby. Can you help us please?' Joseph asked the innkeeper.

That night Jesus was born in a smelly stable surrounded by animals. Mary wrapped him in strips of cloth and laid him in a manger.

FACT
Eastern newborn babies are washed in salted water.

ACTIVITY...
MAKE A POP-UP CARD

You will need:
white cardboard,
felt tips/paint, scissors,
glue/tape,
glitter.

1. Using the picture on page 2, draw the nativity scene onto A5 card. Colour or paint and put aside.
2. Cut flaps out of cardboard and copy small pictures onto flaps (eg: a, b and c). Make crease as shown and glue to the main card.

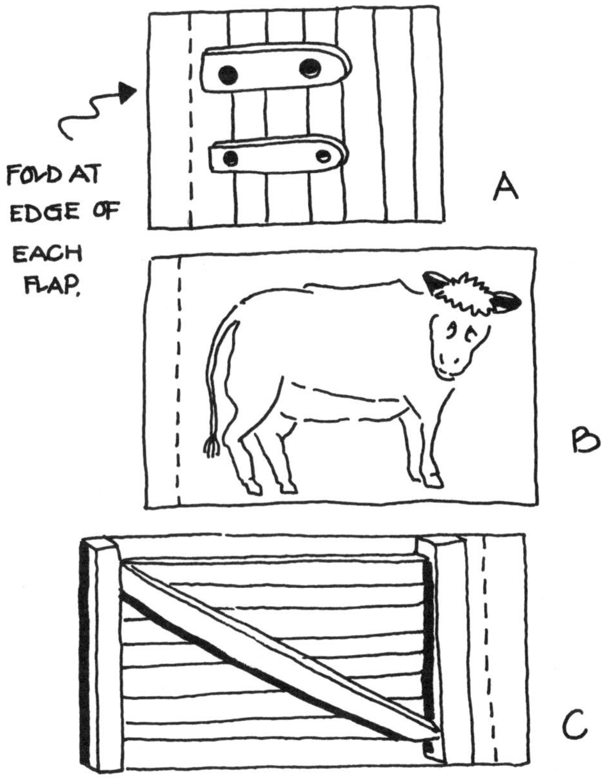

3. Fold a piece of A5 card in half. Draw a star and folds as shown and cut out. Crease fold on the base of the star.

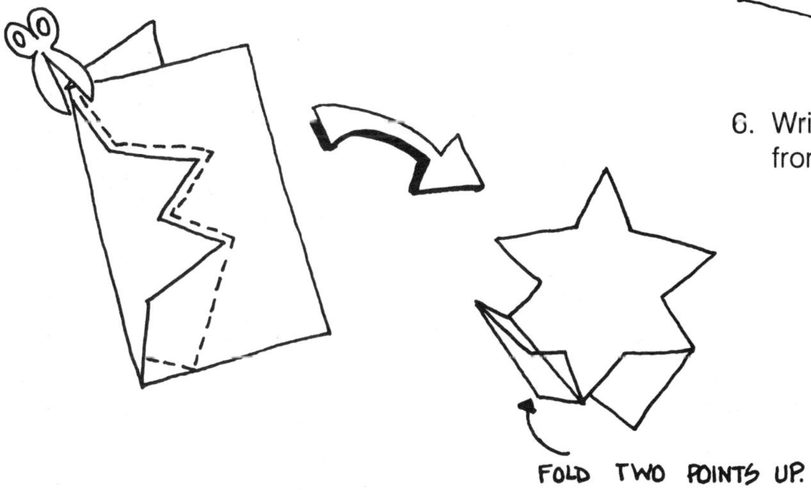

4. Spread glue on star and sprinkle with glitter.

5. Place star in the centre of the card and tape folds on to the card. Star should stand upright when card is opened.

6. Write your own Christmas message on the front of the card.

LEARN ABOUT... JESUS, SAVIOUR OF THE WORLD

This story can be found in the Bible in Luke 2: 8 - 20

The shepherds and their flocks were resting. As they gazed into the starry sky, they could hear the bleating of the sheep. Then suddenly, the night became like day. Brilliant lights shone everywhere.

The shepherds were frightened and didn't know what to do.

'Don't be afraid,' said the angel. 'I bring exciting news . A king is born in Bethlehem. He will save everyone from their sins.'

Some of the shepherds didn't believe.

'Go and you will find the baby wrapped in swaddling clothes, lying in a manger.'

'Look!' shouted a shepherd pointing to the heavens. The sky was filled with angels singing:'Glory to God in the highest. Peace, goodwill to all men everywhere.'

Then it became dark and quiet again. The shepherds raced to Bethlehem as fast as they could. They all wanted to see this special baby that the angels spoke and sang about.

Mary and Joseph were happy to see the shepherds who told them about the angels' visit. The shepherds were overjoyed and spread the good news.

'A king is born! He will save many from their sins,' they told everyone they met. All night they sang praises to God and thought about all they had seen and heard.

FACT
Shepherds carried a sling, club and staff to protect their flock.

ACTIVITY...
MAKE A POSTER

You will need:
coloured foil or wrapping paper, cardboard, scissors, glue, packet of silver stars, cotton wool, string.

1. Cover the top half of the cardboard with blue foil. Cover the bottom half with green foil.

2. Draw sheep, mountains and shepherds on to coloured foil and cut out.

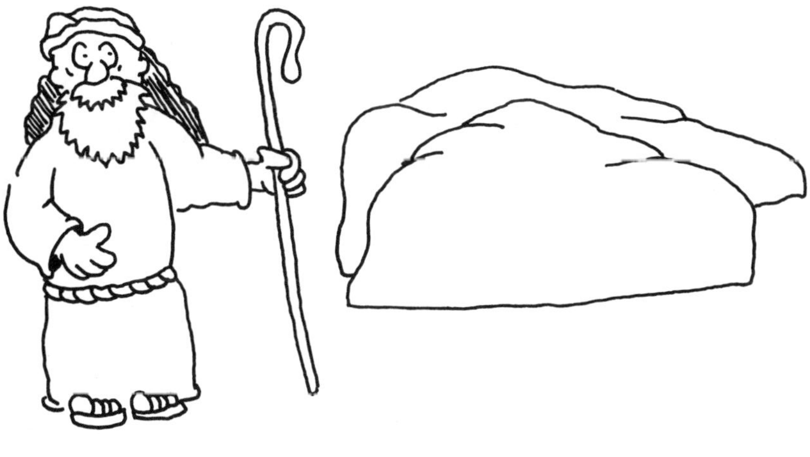

3. Glue the cotton wool onto the sheep. Glue the mountains, and shepherds on to the poster as shown. Stick on the silver stars.

4. Tape string on the back of the poster and hang it on the wall.

LEARN ABOUT... JESUS, FISHER OF MEN

This story can be found in the Bible in Luke 5: 1 - 11

Simon and Andrew were busy cleaning their nets after a busy night fishing.

'Look at that crowd,' said Simon. 'Who is that man coming towards us?'

To their surprise, Jesus wanted to borrow their boat. They pushed it out into the water. And Jesus sat down and taught the people.

When he was finished, he said to Simon, 'Go out further into the deep and drop your nets.' Who did Jesus think he was? All night they had fished and caught nothing.

'Lord we'll try again because you've asked us to.' All of a sudden lots of fish swam into the nets.

'Help us!' shouted Simon to James and John. Jesus watched as the men struggled to keep their boats from sinking.

Simon was amazed at the miracle. 'Go away from me, Lord,' he cried, 'I have done many bad things.'

Jesus smiled, 'Don't be afraid. From now on I want you to catch men, and not fish.' So Simon, Andrew, James and John left their nets and followed Jesus.

FACT
The Lake of Galilee is shaped like a harp.

ACTIVITY...
MAKE A FISH MOBILE

You will need:
varying lengths of cane, cardboard, coloured cellophane (or sweet wrappers) beads, sequins, paste, scissors, pencil, string.

1. Draw 5 fish shapes on to cardboard and cut out.

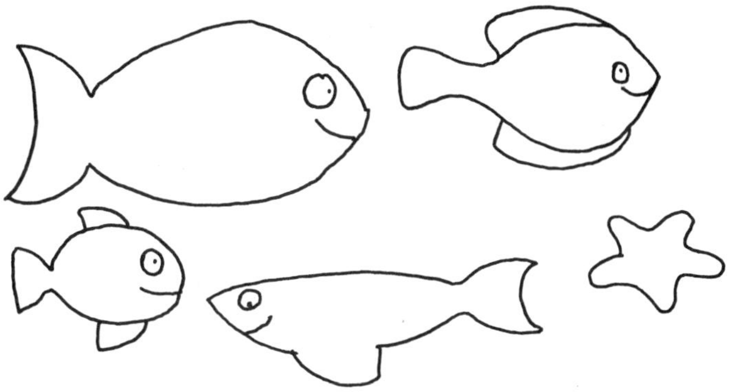

2. Use the cut out fish as templates and draw round them on to the coloured paper.

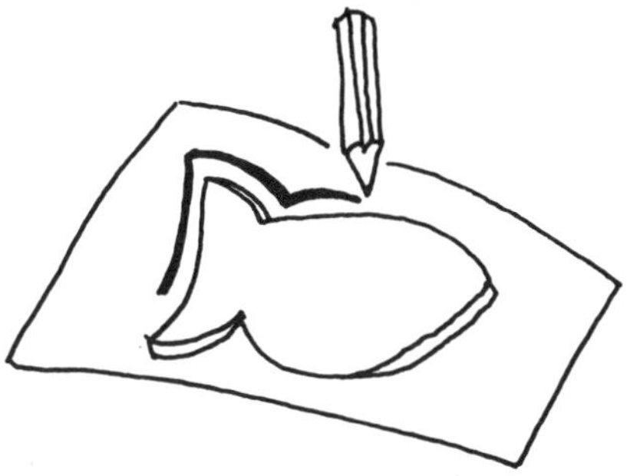

3. Cut out the coloured paper and glue on to the fish shapes.

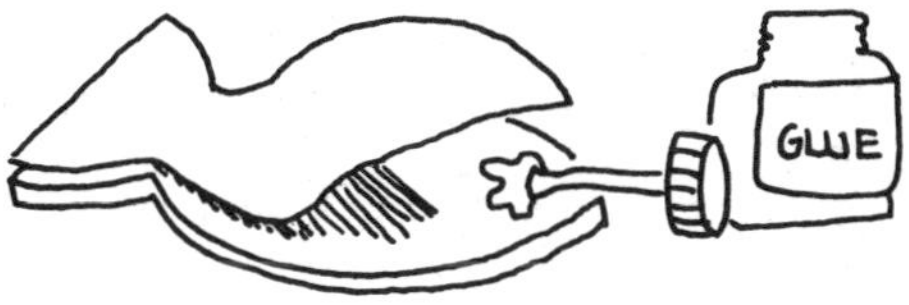

4. Glue large sequins on to fish.

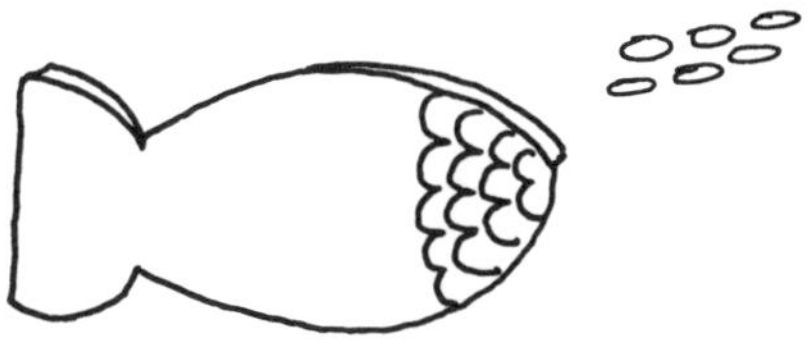

5. Make a pin hole in the top of the fish and tie a piece of string through each shape. (Use various lengths)

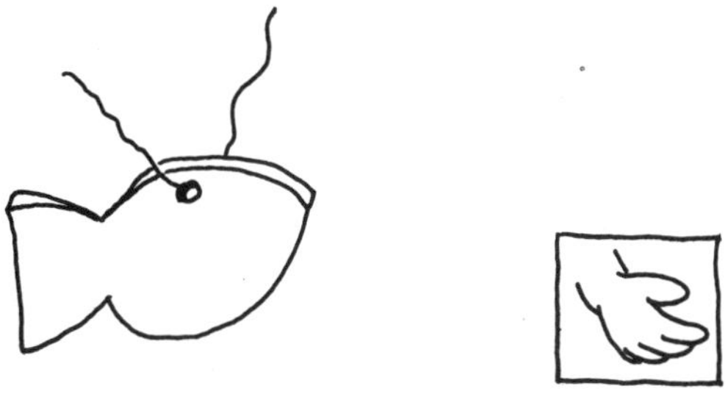

6. Thread beads through the string.

7. Attach the other end of the string to a piece of cane.

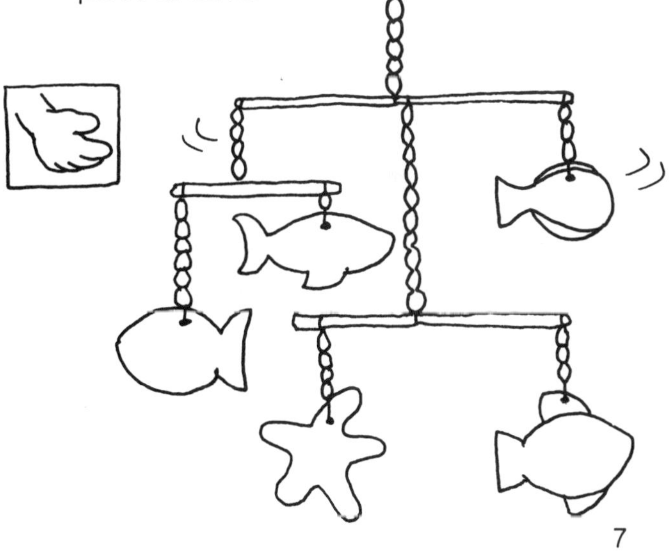

LEARN ABOUT...
JESUS, THE HEALER

This story can be found in the Bible in Luke 5: 17 - 25

'Jesus is here!' shouted the people to one another. Those who were too sick to run, hobbled along. Some were carried by relatives.

Many people expected Jesus to heal the sick. Wonderful stories had been told of his kindness and his amazing miracles.

A house was packed with people who wanted to hear Jesus teach and see his miracles. Four men hurried towards the house. They were carrying a paralysed man on a stretcher but couldn't get in.

'We mustn't give up,' said one man.

They climbed the outside stairs and hoisted the stretcher onto the flat tiled roof. Then they began to break a big hole in the roof.

Crash! Bang! Pieces of tile and wood fell onto the people.

The people gazed at the roof as the four men lowered their friend in front of Jesus. Jesus knew the men believed he would make their friend well again.

'Your sins are forgiven,' declared Jesus. The scribes began thinking in their hearts that Jesus was blaspheming. 'Only God can forgive sins', they thought.

'Which is easier, to say your sins are forgiven or get up and walk?

'To prove I am the Son of God and that I have the power to forgive sins, this man will walk. Get up,' Jesus said. 'Take up your stretcher and go home.'

The man jumped up and did as Jesus told him. The people were astonished. They rejoiced and worshipped God.

But the scribes hated Jesus even more.

FACT
Beds were thin, flexible mattresses that could be rolled up and carried.

ACTIVITY...
MAKE A JIGSAW PUZZLE

You will need:
thin cardboard,
pencil and felt tips,
scissors,
tracing paper.

1. Trace this picture on to the cardboard.
2. Colour it in and then draw straight or zigzag lines all over the picture.
3. Carefully, cut the picture on those lines.
4. Mix up the pieces and put them together to make up the picture.

(1.)

LEARN ABOUT...
JESUS, THE TEACHER

This story can be found in the Bible in Luke 6: 43 - 45

Jesus loved to talk to his twelve apostles about everyday things in life, like money, seeds, animals and fruit.

'A good tree never bears bad fruit. A bad tree never bears good fruit. How do you recognise a tree?'

'By the fruit it bears,' shouted one of his disciples.

'Do you pick figs from thorn bushes? Or do you pick grapes from bramble bushes? No. Therefore a good person stores up lots of good, kind things in his heart. When he speaks, only those things come out of his mouth.

'If you are bad, everyone will know. You will always say bad things and do bad things. What a person says and does, tells you what they are storing up in their heart.' The apostles and the disciples thought about what Jesus was saying.

Do you know what the nine fruits of God's Spirit are? Love, joy, peace, patience, kindness, goodness, faithfulness, gentleness and self-control, these are the fruit of God's Spirit that a Christian should bear.

FACT
Grapes were eaten fresh, dried into raisins or made into wine.

ACTIVITY...
MAKE A FRUIT TREE

You will need:
a leafless branch,
string and paste,
strips of card,
tub of sand,
felt tips / pencils,
tape.

1. Stand branch in tub of sand securely.

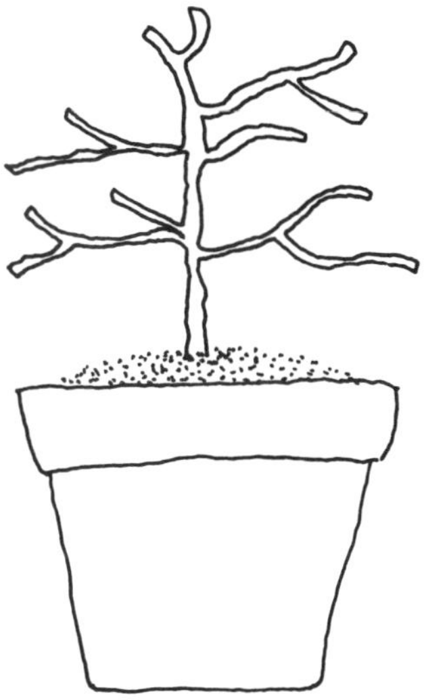

2. Think of nine fruits and draw them on card. Cut out the shapes and write the names of the fruit of the Spirit.

1. 

2. 

3. KINDNESS
4. GENTLENESS
5. FAITHFULNESS
6. PATIENCE
7. JOY
8. GOODNESS
9. SELF CONTROL

3. Tape bits of string to the back of each paper, and hang them on the branch of your tree.

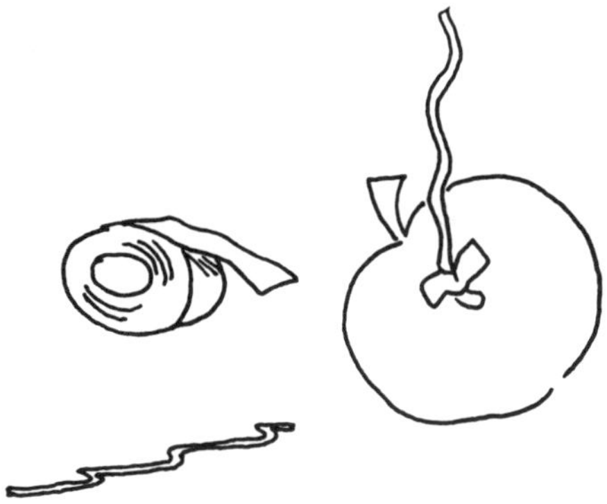

LEARN ABOUT...
JESUS, FRIEND OF SINNERS

This story can be found in the Bible in Luke 6: 27 - 37

The religious rulers hated Jesus because of his amazing miracles and wise words. But most of all, they hated Jesus because he said he was the Son of God.

'This is how you treat your enemies,' said Jesus to his disciples. The people were eager to hear what Jesus had to say. 'Practice doing good things for them. Give to your enemies who are in need. Do not expect them to return what you have given them.

'Sinners love those who love them. They are kind and generous to those who are kind and generous to them. Be different! Love those who hate you and be kind to those who are cruel to you.

'Ask God to bless them. Copy your Father in heaven. He continues loving selfish and wicked people. They hate him; but he loves them still. Your heavenly Father is sympathetic, tender and compassionate towards people who despise him.

'Do not judge and you will not be judged. Don't gather bad and bitter thoughts in your heart towards anyone. Forgive them and you will be forgiven.'

The religious leaders refused to obey Jesus' words. Instead, they stored up wicked thoughts in their hearts against him.

FACT
Disciples were first called Christians in Antioch.

ACTIVITY...
MAKE A BOUQUET OF FLOWERS

Flowers

1. Copy patterns as shown on to crepe paper.

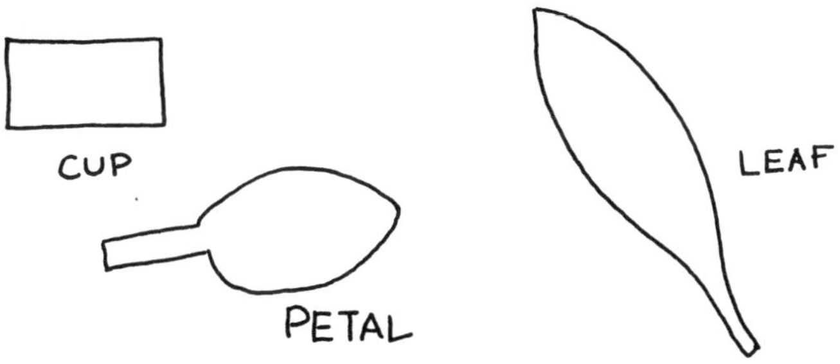

2. Cut small vertical lines at the top of pattern 'A' to create fringes. Shape into a cup and tape to the pipe cleaner.

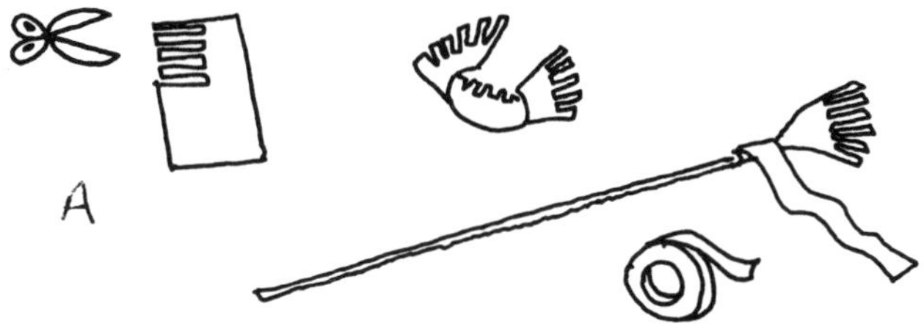

3. Cut six petals from the pattern. Tape these evenly around the base of the cup. Now turn them upwards.

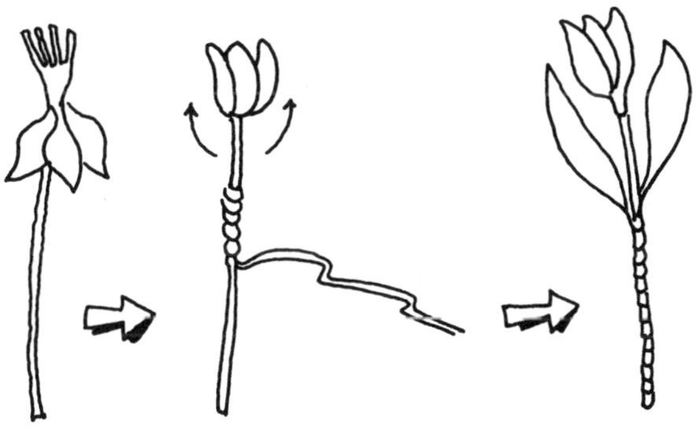

4. Wrap pipe cleaner with green paper and secure with tape.
5. Cut three leaves from the pattern. Tape around the stem. Make several tulips for the bouquet.

You will need:
Crepe paper, paint, pipe cleaner, scissors, glue, sequins, glitter, cardboard, tape.

Butterfly

1. Draw a butterfly on strong white cardboard and cut out.
2. Paint silver or any bright colour. For antennae use black pipe cleaners.
3. Decorate with sequins or glitter.
4. Wrap a pipe cleaner around a pencil for spiral effect.
5. Glue butterfly to spiral and place in the bouquet.

LEARN ABOUT... JESUS, GIVER OF LIFE

This story can be found in the Bible in Luke 7: 11 - 17

The mourners walked towards the city gate. Some were rolling in the dirt and weeping. Some sang sad songs and threw dirt on their heads. Others ripped off their ordinary clothes. They put on a coarse material called sack cloth, and then sat in the ashes weeping. Even those carrying the coffin were crying.

'Oh! Alas! My only son!' wept the widow. 'No husband and no son,' she cried out as she beat her breast with her hands. 'Who will look after me?'

Everyone felt sorry for her. As Jesus and his disciples approached Nain, they saw the funeral procession and the widow weeping. Jesus felt compassion for her. He wanted to make her joyful again.

'Don't cry,' he said, walking to the coffin.

'Why doesn't he let the woman bury her son?'

'Has he come to laugh at her and cause her more sorrow?'

'Young man, I say to you, get up!' commanded Jesus.

He sat up straight away and talked with Jesus. His mother hugged and kissed her son.

She began to sing because Jesus had turned her mourning into rejoicing. Everyone stopped weeping too. They sang praises to God for his kindness to the widow. 'God has come to help his people,' they sang.

And the news of the miracle spread throughout Judea.

FACT
Rich families employed professional mourners to weep loudly and sing sad songs.

ACTIVITY...
MAKE HAND PUPPETS

You will need:
one piece of coloured felt 23 x 28 cm,
pins, thread and needle,
scraps of felt for face,
fabric glue.

1. Cut two mitten shapes out of a large piece of felt and pin the pieces together.

2. Sew around the edges - leave room for your hand to go in. Watch those fingers!

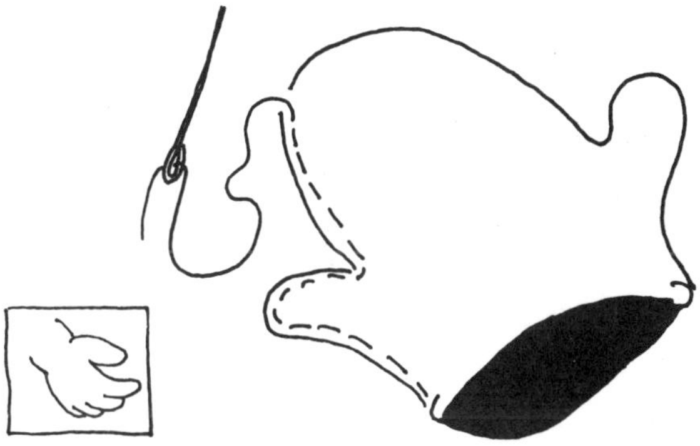

3. Cut out the eyes, ears, mouth, beard and nose from the scraps of felt. Glue or sew on to puppet.

4. Cut out and glue on extra piece for head dress.

LEARN ABOUT... JESUS, THE FARMER

This story can be found in the Bible in Luke 8: 4 - 15

'A farmer went out to sow seeds,' said Jesus teaching the people and his apostles. 'The farmer walked up and down scattering handfuls of seeds over the field.

'Some fell on the path and the birds ate them up. Some fell on stony patches. The soil was shallow, but the seedlings still grew quickly. When the sun came out, those seedlings withered and died because there was no moisture.

'Some seeds fell among thorn bushes. As they grew, the thorns choked them. The rest of the seeds fell on good soil, which grew strong and produced hundreds of fruit.'

'What did that parable mean, Jesus?' asked the disciples.

'The seed is God's word. Some hear it, but as soon as they hear it, the devil steals the word from their hearts. Others hear and believe the word. They are happy for a while, but when they are faced with troubles or problems, they doubt the word and turn away from God.

'The worldly hearers give riches and their own desires first place. Soon the word of God is forgotten. Some people,' continued Jesus, 'are like the seeds that fell on good soil. They listen to the word and do as it says. Soon they become strong Christians and they lead others into the kingdom of God.'

FACT
Eastern children enjoyed pretending to be scarecrows.

ACTIVITY...
MAKE A HAIRY SPIDER

You will need:
ice-cream tub,
coloured paper,
crayons, tape,
grass seeds,
soil / compost.

1. Draw friendly spider face on paper.
   Tape around tub.

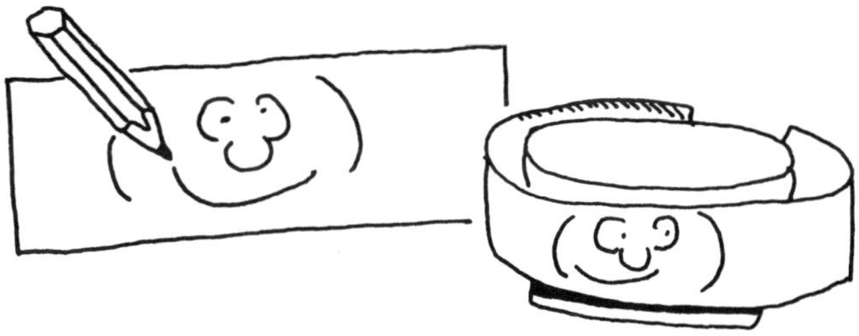

2. Put soil / compost in tub. Pour in enough
   water to make it moist.

3. Sprinkle grass seeds evenly over surface.

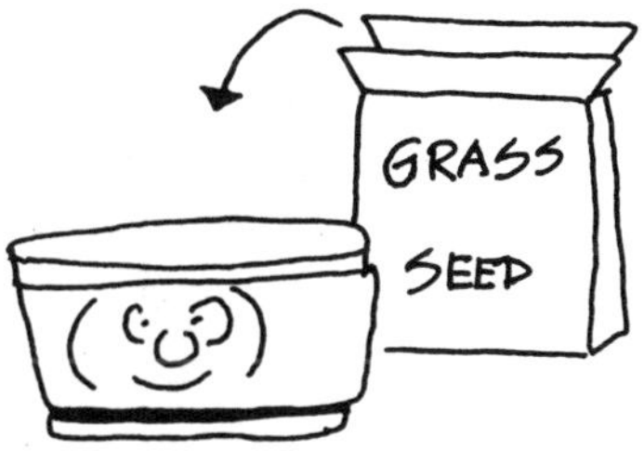

4. Cover with more soil / compost.

5. Fold eights strips of paper for legs.
   Glue on to the tub.

6. Place hairy spider on window sill. Water
   regularly. Grass will be lush in 4 weeks.
   Trim hairy spider's hair to keep it tidy.

LEARN ABOUT...
JESUS, BREAD OF LIFE

This story is found in the Bible in Luke 9: 10 - 17

As soon as the people heard that Jesus had gone to Bethsaida, they followed him. He was very glad to see them. After teaching about God's kingdom, he healed those who were sick.

As evening approached, the people became hungry and tired .

'Send them away to nearby towns to buy food and find places to sleep,' said the disciples to Jesus.

'You give them something to eat,' declared Jesus. What should they do? They would have to go to nearby towns and buy food. But where would they find food for over 5,000 people? All they had were five loaves and two fishes that a little boy had given them.

'This is all we have,' they said showing Jesus the lunch.

Jesus told them to seat the people in groups of fifty. Then he took the loaves and fishes from the disciples and blessed the food. Afterwards, Jesus broke the fish and the bread and gave it to the disciples. They distributed it among the hungry crowd. They were amazed because there was enough food for everyone.

There were even twelve baskets left over. The people rejoiced because Jesus had miraculously fed them.

FACT
Fish can be dried and salted for storing.

ACTIVITY...
MAKE PANCAKES

You will need:
2 eggs, 2¼ cups
plain flour, 1 tsp. salt,
2 cups of milk, 1 tsp. sugar,
2 tsp. baking powder, sprinkle of
nutmeg, butter,
½ tsp. of vanilla
flavouring, oil,
1 tsp. sugar.

1. Mix the flour, sugar, salt, baking powder and nutmeg together in a bowl.

2. Beat eggs in another bowl. Add milk and vanilla flavouring.

3. Pour milk mixture into the flour mixture and stir gently.

4. Melt some butter in a pan and add to the mixture, stirring gently.

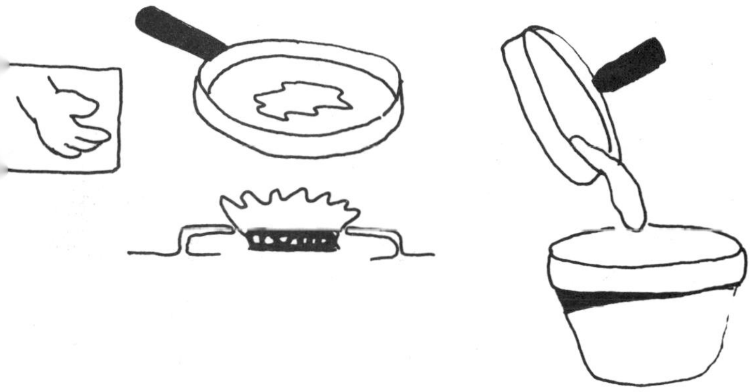

5. Put a little oil in frying pan / girdle. When it is hot, pour 2 tablespoons of mixture into the frying pan.

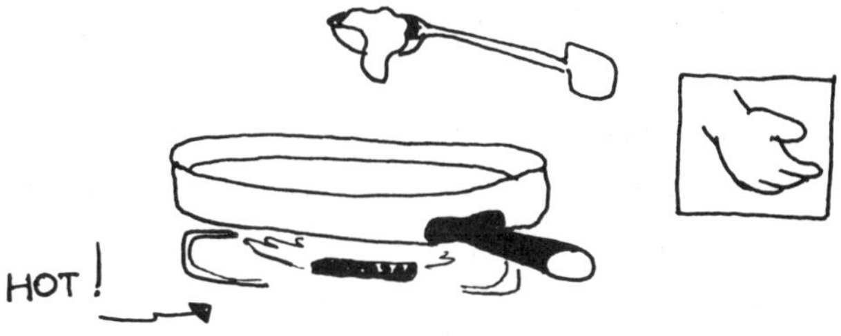

6. Bubbles will appear. Turn pancakes when the bubbles pop.

7. Remove when middle of pancake is cooked.
8. Serve with butter and jam or maple syrup.

LEARN ABOUT...
JESUS, THE SHEPHERD

This story can be found in the Bible in Luke 15: 1 - 7

Jesus loved talking to and listening to the people. Sometimes he would visit drunks, prostitutes, and other social outcasts. This made the religious leaders angry and they hated him even more. But Jesus wasn't bothered. He still talked to them.

'Tell us about God's kingdom, Jesus,' the people cheered.

'A man has 100 sheep and one gets lost in the wilderness. What should he do? Should he take the 99 sheep back home and leave the other one to die? Or should he leave the 99 sheep somewhere safe and go and search for the lost sheep?' The people discussed this among themselves.

'The shepherd must search everywhere until he finds the sheep. Otherwise a wild animal may eat it.

'Yes. And when he finds his sheep, he will place it on his shoulders and go home rejoicing,' said Jesus.

The religious leaders looked puzzled, 'Who cares about one lost sheep?'

'God does. Everyone is important to God. It doesn't matter how good or bad they have been.'

FACT
Some shepherds comforted their flocks by playing a flute.

ACTIVITY...
MAKE A FLUFFY SHEEP

You will need:
White cotton wool balls, toilet roll tube, glue, 2 pipe cleaners, white paint, crepe paper or old tights.

1. Take a pipe cleaner and pierce 4 holes in the toilet roll tube. Insert each pipe cleaner through the tube as shown and bend for feet.

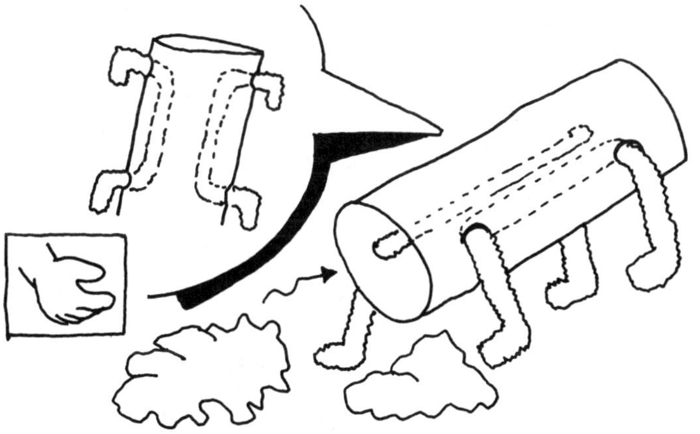

2. Fill the tube with crepe paper, leaving room for cotton wool to be added. Cover the outside of the tube with glue.

3. Fluff out cotton wool balls and stick on to the tube until it is covered. Fill both ends with cotton wool balls.

4. Take a piece of black crepe paper or an old piece of tights and wrap up a cotton ball, tying or twisting at the ends to make ears.

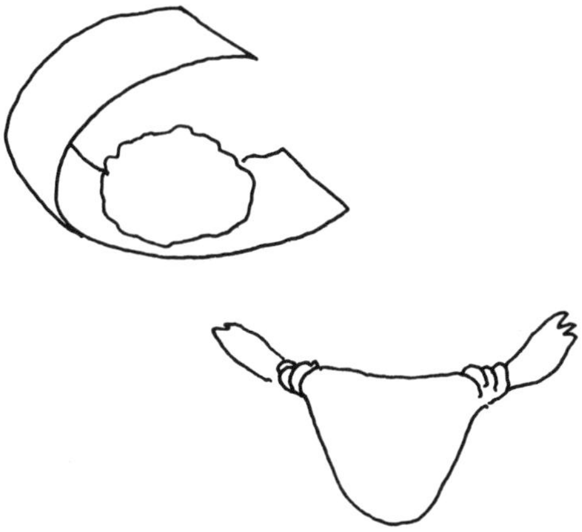

5. Use white paint to make the face and glue the head to the body, packing with cotton wool to make secure.

LEARN ABOUT...
JESUS, THE KING

This story is found in the Bible in Luke 19: 28 - 38

Many people were travelling to Jerusalem. They were very excited. Soon it would be time to celebrate Passover.

During Passover the Jews remembered how God brought them safely out of Egypt when they were slaves.

Jesus and his disciples were also going to Jerusalem. 'In the village you will see a young donkey tied beside its mother. Bring it to me,' said Jesus.

The disciples went to the village. 'What are you doing?' asked the owner.

'The Master needs it,' they said, placing their coats on the donkey. 'Don't worry we will return it.'

The disciples were unhappy and confused. Jesus told them he would die and rise again after three days. How could this happen? They wanted him to be King.

The children sang and waved palm branches as Jesus passed by. Some people spread the branches on the road. Others threw their coats on the road for the donkey to walk over.

'Hosanna!' they shouted. 'Blessed is he who comes in the name of the Lord!' others cheered.

Many believed he was the Messiah. Was he going to be the King of Israel as the Holy books had declared?

When the chief priests heard of the celebrations, they were angry and jealous. 'We must stop him,' they said. 'He will turn the people against us.'

'We must make a plan to trap and kill him.' snarled another.

FACT
During Old Testament times, it was common for kings to ride donkeys or mules.

ACTIVITY...
MAKE A DONKEY

You will need:
five pipe cleaners,
crayons, glue,
small piece of
cardboard.

1. Bend two pipe cleaners into 'U' shapes.

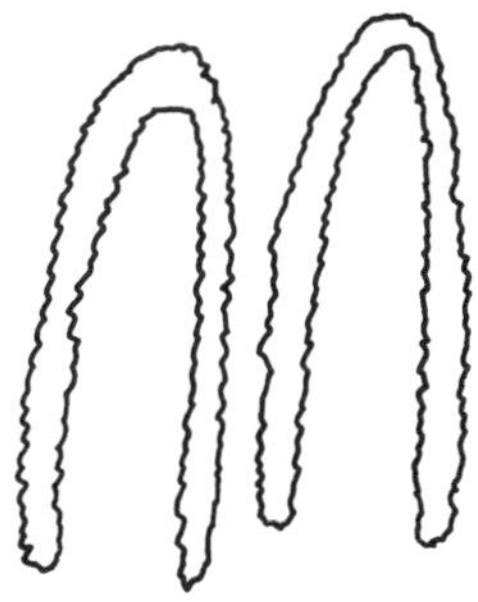

2. Put the 'U' shaped pipe cleaners together to make the front and back legs.

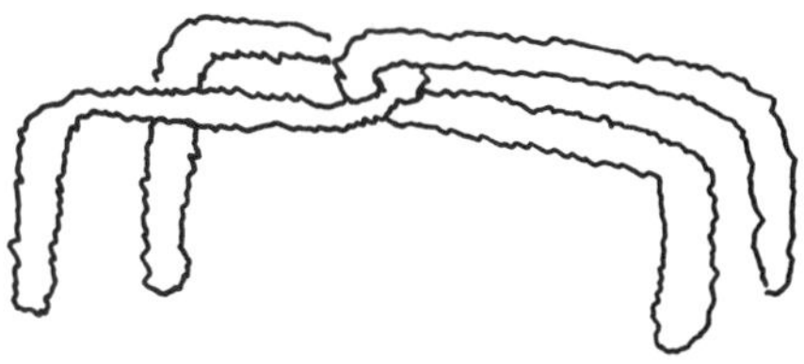

3. Bend another pipe cleaner upwards at both ends to make the neck and tail.

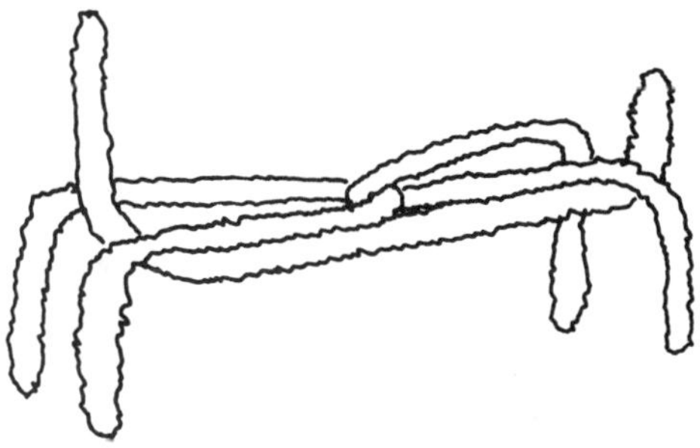

4. Wrap another pipe cleaner around the body, while holding the third pipe cleaner in position.

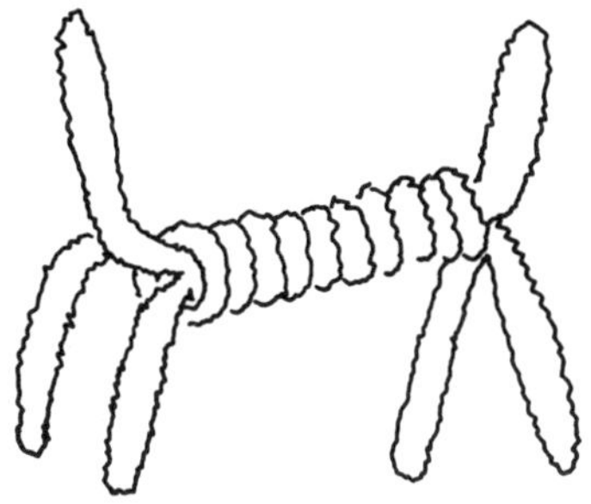

5. Tie a small piece of pipe cleaner around the neck to make the ears.

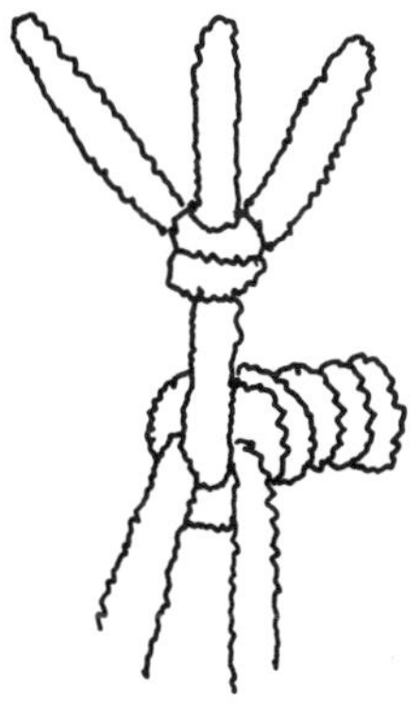

6. Turn the neck down or glue a piece of cardboard onto the neck to make a head. Draw and colour a face.

LEARN ABOUT...
JESUS, THE SERVANT

This story can be found in the Bible in Luke 22:1 - 34 & John 13:1 -17

The chief priests and scribes hated Jesus so much they wanted to kill him. They decided to wait until after Passover. Judas Iscariot, one of the twelve went to the chief priests secretly and agreed to help them catch Jesus.

Meanwhile, Jesus had sent John and Peter into the city. He told them they would see a man carrying a water pitcher. They should follow him home.

'Ask him and he will tell you where the Master and his disciples will celebrate Passover. Go to the upstairs room and prepare the feast.'

After supper, Jesus began washing their feet. They were astonished. 'Surely, this is a servant's job.'

'Follow my example and serve others as I do,' Jesus said. During the meal the disciples talked and ate.

Jesus broke bread and poured wine, which he passed to the disciples. 'This is our last meal together for now, so eat bread and drink wine as a way of remembering me.

'It is time for me to suffer. My betrayer sits with me at the table,' Jesus said sadly. The disciples wondered who among them would do such a thing.

'I would never betray you, Lord. I am ready to go to prison and to die for you,' declared Peter.

'Before the rooster crows,' replied Jesus, 'you will deny that you ever knew me three times.'

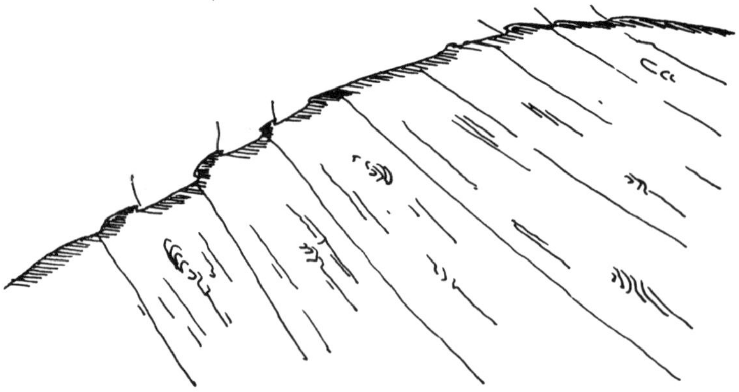

FACT
It was customary for Jews to wash their visitor's feet.

ACTIVITY...
MAKE A FRUIT SALAD PORTRAIT

1. Cut grapes in half. Use them to make the outline of a face.

2. Slice banana and apple into thin strips. Sprinkle lemon juice on banana and apple to prevent discolouration.

3. Use three banana slices for eyebrows and nose. Use an apple slice for the mouth.

4. Slice kiwi and orange thinly. Cut an orange slice in half. One half for each ear. Use kiwi slices for eyes.

You will need:
banana, apple, orange, grapes, kiwi, (or seasonal fruits) & liquorice.

5. Cut liquorice into strips and use for hair.

6. Use leftover grapes to fill out the face. Use orange and banana slices for the shoulders.

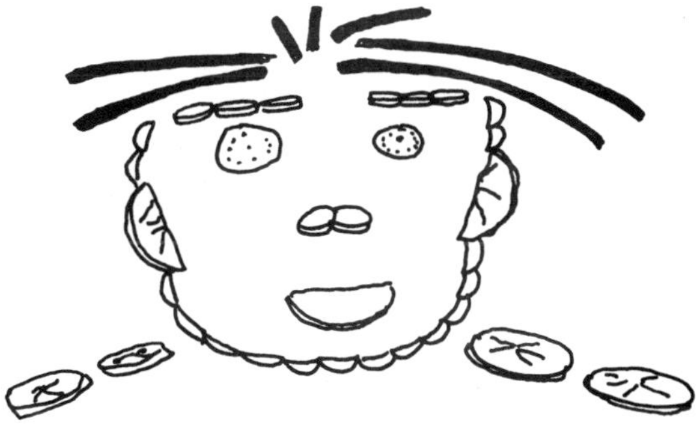

7. Experiment using dried fruits or vegetables for another portrait.

LEARN ABOUT...
JESUS, THE PERFECT MAN

This story can be found in the Bible in Luke 22: 47 - 62

Judas Iscariot ran ahead of the religious leaders and the soldiers. He kissed Jesus on the cheek.

'Will you betray me with a kiss, Judas,' asked Jesus. His disciples realised what would happen next and one of them chopped off the High Priest's servant's ear. Everyone watched as Jesus restored the servant's ear.

'Why have you brought clubs and swords? You saw me daily in the temple. Why didn't you take me then?'

They led him to the High Priest's house. Peter followed far behind and waited outside. The High Priest was eager to convict Jesus of crimes that would cause his death. Many people agreed to testify against Jesus by lying.

In the courtyard of the High Priest's house, the people huddled around the fire to keep warm. Peter noticed a servant girl staring at him.

'There's one of his friends,' she said pointing to Peter.

'I don't know him,' replied Peter angrily. Soon after that someone else recognised him. Once again, he denied knowing Jesus.

An hour later Peter was still waiting for news of Jesus. 'I am sure that this man was with him,' said someone, 'he is a Galilean.'

'I tell you, I do not know what you are talking about.' 'Cock-a-doodle-doo!' crowed the rooster. Jesus turned and gazed at Peter. Peter left the courtyard weeping bitterly because he had denied his friend.

FACT
Names of children are chosen to reflect their character eg: Jonah means 'dove'.

ACTIVITY...
MAKE A ROOSTER

You will need:
card, coloured felt,
needle and thread,
glue, stuffing eg:
cotton wool or
old tights.

1. Copy these shapes on to card.
   Cut them out and pin on to pieces of felt.

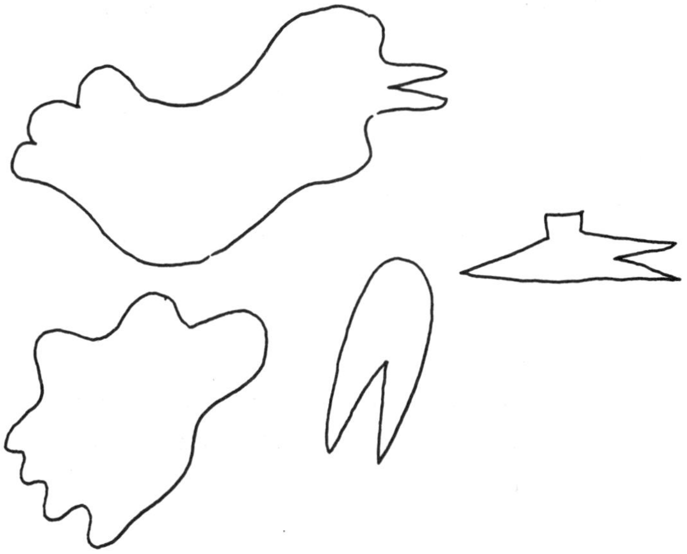

2. Cut out two sets of felt shapes. Use different colours for different parts of the body.
3. Sew the rooster's comb, feet and wings on to the body. Cut circles for eyes and glue on to felt.

4. Sew the body together, leaving an opening for stuffing.

5. Stuff rooster with cotton balls or pieces of cloth or old tights until the body is firm. Stitch up the opening.

LEARN ABOUT... JESUS, LAMB OF GOD

This story can be found in the Bible in Luke 23: 1 - 49

The religious rulers took Jesus to Pilate because only Roman rulers had the power to issue death sentences. Pilate could find nothing wrong with him. He ordered the soldiers to take him to Herod who was in charge of Galilee.

Herod had hoped to see an amazing miracle, but Jesus did none. So he sent Jesus back to Pilate.

'He has done nothing wrong,' declared Pilate, 'I'll whip him and release him.'

'Give us Barabbas, the murderer! Kill Jesus!' the crowds chanted angrily.

'Jesus is innocent . . . '

'. . . No! Crucify Jesus. Let Barabbas live.' Pilate did as the people said.

As Jesus stumbled on the way to Calvary, the soldiers forced a man called Simon to carry the cross.

The crowds cheered as the soldiers placed a crown of thorns upon his head and ripped off his clothes.

'You don't look like a king now,' laughed the scribes. The soldiers hammered Jesus' hands and feet to the cross.

After lifting up the cross they pushed it into the ground.

'Save yourself and us,' sneered one of the criminals beside him.

'We are guilty but Jesus is innocent,' spoke the other man, and turning to Jesus said 'Remember me in heaven.'

'You will be there,' replied Jesus. As the sun grew dark the temple veil split in two. Jesus cried out to God to receive his spirit and then died.

The religious leaders laughed. Had they seen the last of Jesus?

FACT
Pens were made from reeds and rushes which were sharpened by knives.

ACTIVITY...
MAKE A SCROLL & PRINTING PRESS

You will need:
paper,
2 kitchen roll tubes,
felt tips, pencil,
ribbon, knife,
paint, potatoes.

1. Cut a piece of paper to fit the length of a kitchen roll tube. Write the message on the scroll below. (Remember to leave enough space at the top and bottom to wrap around kitchen rolls.)

2. Glue the ends of your paper and wrap round the kitchen roll tube and put aside to dry.

3. Cut a large potato in half. Mark out your design with a pen.

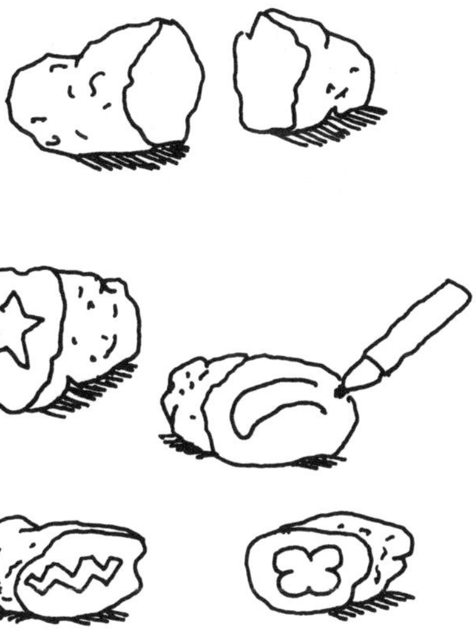

4. Cut around your design to the depth of about 20mm.

5. Dip in paint and stamp at the bottom of your scroll.

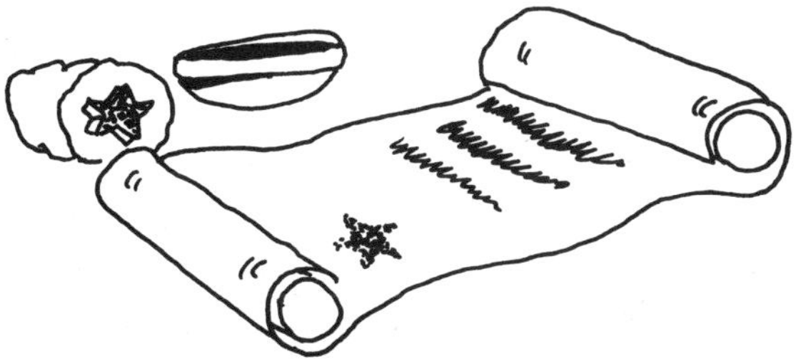

6. Tie with a ribbon and give to someone as a gift.

PS: Why not write a coded message to a friend?

LEARN ABOUT...
JESUS, HE'S ALIVE!

This story can be found in the Bible in Luke 24: 1 - 12

Mary was heartbroken since Jesus' death. Early on the Sunday morning, a few women who loved Jesus went to the tomb. Mary carried spices to sprinkle on Jesus' clothes.

When they arrived at the tomb the women couldn't believe their eyes. Someone had moved the heavy stone. Mary ran quickly to the tomb. She looked in and saw two angels sitting down.

'Why are you looking for Jesus in a tomb? He is risen!' said the angels. 'Remember he told you he would die and then rise on the third day?'

Meanwhile, the disciples were hiding in a locked room. They were sad and afraid. They thought that the priests would kill them too.

The women ran to the house where the disciples were hiding.

'He's alive!' Mary shouted. 'He's risen.'

'Nonsense. We saw him crucified,' said a disciple.

'Do you remember he told us he would die and then rise on the third day?' While the women tried to convince the disciples that Jesus was alive, Peter ran to the tomb to see for himself.

'Wouldn't it be wonderful if he was alive,' Peter thought to himself.

FACT
Jewish children played games similar to tug of war and hockey.

ACTIVITY...
MAKE A DANCING PERSON

You will need:
115mm strip of card,
Coloured thread,
Needle,
String, wool,
cane.

1. Wrap wool 40 times around the card.

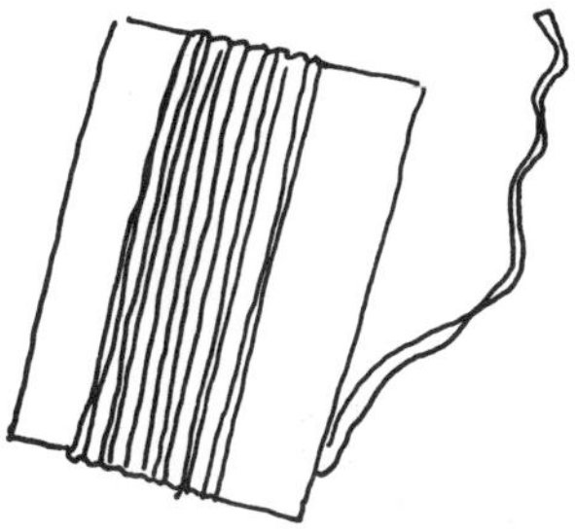

2. Tie wool at one end with thread and cut the other end carefully. Put card aside.

3. Tie the hands, waist and neck with coloured thread. Cut arms at required length and tie legs for man.

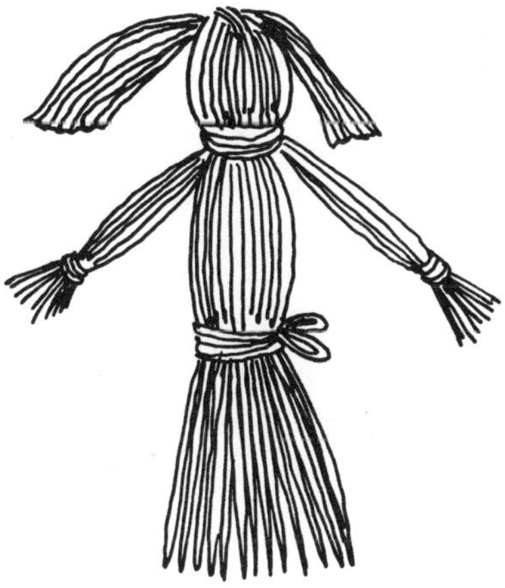

4. For the dancing person's eyes, nose and mouth, use needle and thread to sew three dots and a curved line.

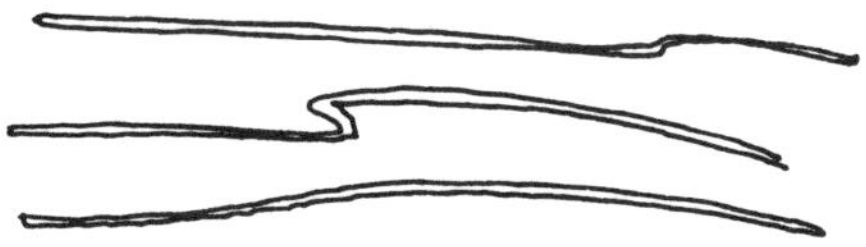

5. Cut string into three equal parts. Tie a piece of string to both wrists and top of the head.
6. Tie the other end of the string to a piece of cane and make him/her dance by pulling the strings.

LEARN ABOUT...
JESUS, THE COMING KING

This story can be found in Luke 24: 36 - 53 and Acts 1: 3 - 11

Later, Jesus appeared to his friends.

'It's a g-g-ghost,' one disciple whimpered. Jesus let them touch his wounds just to prove that he was flesh and bones. They were amazed as Jesus ate some broiled fish.

Afterwards Jesus talked with them. 'I have accomplished what my Father sent me to do. Now everyone can receive forgiveness for their sins. Go everywhere, and preach about the forgiveness of sins. Tell them God loves them.'

'He speaks as though he is going away again,' thought one disciple.

'Go to Jerusalem and wait for the promise of the Father. The Holy Spirit will fill you with power to witness,' said Jesus.

After he had blessed them, the disciples watched as Jesus began rising towards heaven, surrounded by clouds.

'Will he come back?' asked a disciple.

'This same Jesus, shall come back again,' said two angels. 'In the same way he went up to heaven.'

The disciples left and went to Jerusalem to wait for the promise of the Holy Spirit.

ACTIVITY...
MAKE A POT-POURRI DOVE

You will need:
cloth, cardboard,
fabric glue / tape,
needle, thread,
scissors, pot-pourri,
ribbon, paper.

1. Draw dove pattern on to paper. Pin to cloth and cut out.
2. Sew around the edges of the dove. Leave an opening. Gently stuff pot-pourri into the body of the dove and close opening.
3. Draw two diamonds or hearts on card board as shown.Cut out shaded areas.
4. Use strips of cloth to wrap around the shape. Secure with fabric glue or tape.
5. Use needle and thread to hang the dove in the diamond / heart.
6. Glue or sew a piece of looped ribbon at the top of the heart and hang it in window.

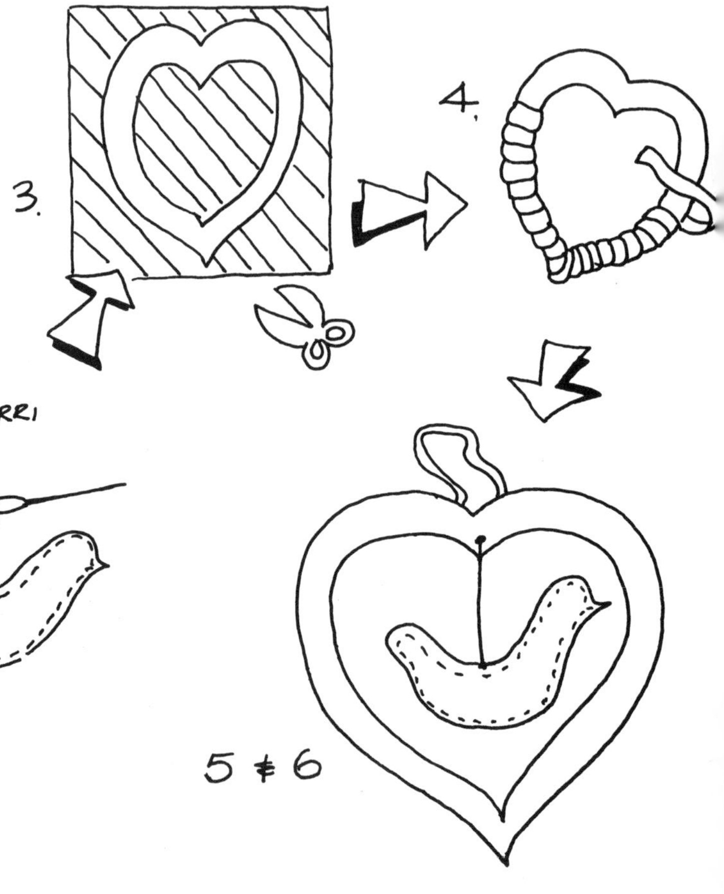

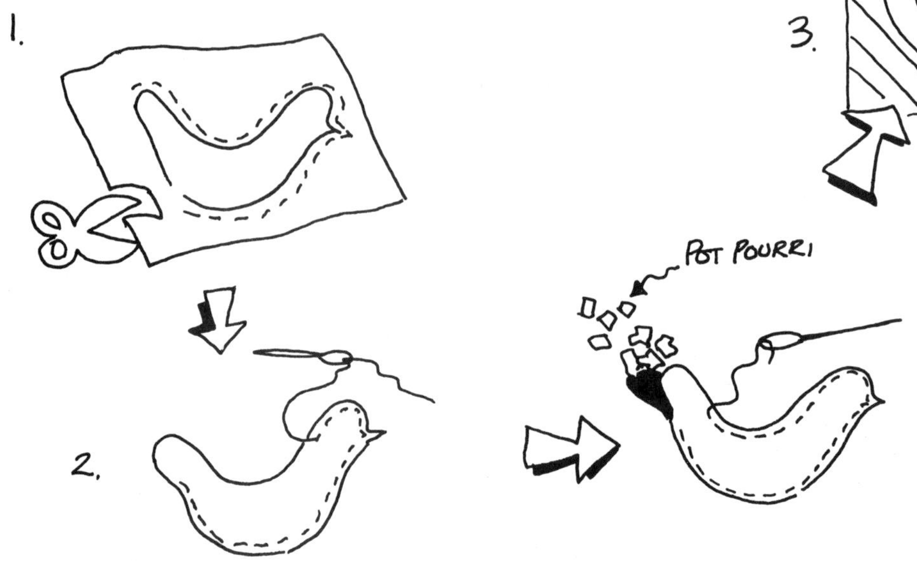